DUAL ENROLLMENT HANDBOOK

10 STEPS To Enroll High School Students In Concurrent Classes At California Community Colleges

Jeannie Karlitz

Earn Both High School And College Credits For Free!   **Simultaneously**

Online Or In-Person

Copyright © 2020 Jeannie Karlitz

No part of this book may be reproduced, or stored in a retrieval system, or transmitted in any form or by any means, electronic, mechanical, photocopying, recording, or otherwise, without express written permission of the author.

Printed in the United States of America

CONTENTS

Title Page	
Copyright	
Abbreviations	1
Dual Enrollment Explained	2
Dual enrollmEnt History in California	3
Advantages of Dual enrollment Classes	4
Disadvantages of Dual enrollment Classes	5
Dual enrollment classes versus Adavanced placement and International Baccalaureate classes	6
College Credits and Transferability	7
Grade point averages and Transcripts	8
FERPA, 504s and IEPs	10
Financial Responsibilities	11
Browse and Search for DUAL ENROLLMENT Classes	12
10 STEPS to Register for Dual Enrollment Classes	15
Appendix	18
About the Author	21

ABBREVIATIONS

AP: Advanced Placement

CCAP: California Career Access Pathways

CCC: California Community College

CSU: California State University

DuE: Dual Enrollment

ECHS: Early College High Schools

FERPA: The Family Educational Rights and Privacy Act of 1974

GE: General Education

GPA: Grade Point Average

IB: International Baccalaureate

IEP: Individualized Education Program

IGETC: Intersegmental General Education Transfer Curriculum

UC: University of California

504: Section 504 of the Rehabilitation Act of 1973

DUAL ENROLLMENT EXPLAINED

Dual enrollment (DuE), also referred to as a concurrent enrollment, is when high school students are dually enrolled in high school and community college. DuE classes are community college classes, with enrolled high school students who can receive high school and college credits simultaneously.

DuE classes are typically taught by a community college professor, online, in-person on the community college campus, or in-person on a partner high school campus. If the DuE class is provided through a partner high school it is only available to students attending that specific partner high school. Additionally, DuE classes run by partner high schools can be taught by a high school teacher or a partner community college professor.

DUAL ENROLLMENT HISTORY IN CALIFORNIA

DuE classes were initially intended to reduce barriers to higher education pathways for low-income and/or underrepresented minority students in California. The results were so positive that DuE classes increased in popularity for all high school students regardless of race or economics. Today, some low-income and/or underserved minority high school students enroll in California Career Access Pathways (CCAP), programs located on California Community College (CCC) campuses, called Early College High Schools (ECHSs) or Middle Colleges where students work in small settings. Most high school students, pursuing college level credit course work, enroll in DuE classes at one or more of the 116 CCCs. High school guidance counselors in high performing schools do not always recommended DuE classes at CCCs to their students. This advice often benefits the high schools, but not the students, as they are encouraged to keep students enrolled in high school classes so they can receive the maximum federal funding.

ADVANTAGES OF DUAL ENROLLMENT CLASSES

The great variety of DuE classes have academic rigor that may help students ease the transition to college. California high school students will accumulate college credits for free when passing DuE classes. DuE classes also fulfill University of California (UC) breadth classes (the UC term for general education classes), or general education (GE) classes at private and out-of-state universities. Careful planning may allow some students to graduate early from a four year institution. UC and Cal State University (CSU) schools award an honors credit for most DuE classes when reviewing applications for admission. Additionally, high school students, in any grade, can explore possible college majors before they enroll as a full-time college student.

DISADVANTAGES OF DUAL ENROLLMENT CLASSES

Some AP courses may be considered more rigorous to college admissions than DuE classes. If students do not do well in DuE classes, the low grades can be on their permanent high school transcript. Additionally, future financial-aid and NCAA eligibility might be affected so it is very important to discuss DuE classes with high school counselors prior to enrolling. Some credits for DuE classes may not transfer to all institutions of higher education therefore careful planning is required. Lastly, students concerned with their weighted grade point averages (GPAs) might not choose to enroll in DuE classes.

DUAL ENROLLMENT CLASSES VERSUS ADAVANCED PLACEMENT AND INTERNATIONAL BACCALAUREATE CLASSES

College credits for Advanced Placement (AP) classes and International Baccalaureate (IB) classes are not guaranteed. Both AP and IB classes require an exam for each class to be considered for college credits. DuE classes are guaranteed to transfer as college credits to at least one California institution of higher education. However, UCs, CSUs, and private institutions do not accept all the same DuE classes as each university has different transferability criteria.

COLLEGE CREDITS AND TRANSFERABILITY

College credits earned from DuE classes can transfer to four year colleges and universities with careful planning. UC breadth credits, also referred to as The Intersegmental General Education Transfer Curriculum (IGETC) credits, and college elective credits, can be earned through DuE classes. Steps to confirm transferability are explained further in **Browse and Search for DuE Classes.**

High school students can earn a maximum of 11 credits through DuE classes per semester. Students in California Career Access Pathways (CCAP) can earn a maximum of 15 credits, in 4 courses or less, per semester.

GRADE POINT AVERAGES AND TRANSCRIPTS

Required high school courses may be replaced with DuE classes. For example, *High School World History,* or *World History AP,* have corresponding classes at California Community Colleges. Additionally, the IGETC class, *World History from 1500 - Present,* fulfills the required California *High School World History* class . High School students earn credit bearing letter grades from DuE classes that can be incorporated in high school transcripts. Some schools that use a 5.0 grading scale may place a value of 4.0 on an "A" earned in DuE classes instead of a 5.0 for an "A" earned in AP classes.

For DuE classes that do not fulfill high school requirements, students can choose to leave the classes off their high school transcripts and use the credits earned only towards college credits. Many high schools limit the number of credits students can receive from other institutions, including CCCs. If students do not include their DuE classes on their high school transcripts, the CCC credits earned for those classes may still be transferable to four year institutions of higher education but will not fulfill any high school requirements.

The DuE classes equivalent to California high school A-G classes will receive a honors point when calculated using the UC formula for admissions. UCs and CSUs require transcripts from CCCs in addition to students' high school transcripts.

UCs, CSUs, and most private schools, will consider all students that are dually enrolled in high school and CCCs to be freshman applicants and not transfer students. There is no limit on how many DuE classes students can earn while in high school as long as the DuE credits are earned before high school graduation.

FERPA, 504S AND IEPS

The Family Educational Rights and Privacy Act of 1974 (FERPA or the Buckley Amendment) and Section 504 of the Rehabilitation Act of 1973 gives parents of students under the age of 18 the rights to access their children's records. However, under FERPA, parents do not have those rights for their students over the age of 18. Nevertheless, all institutions of higher education follow the FERPA laws pertaining to students over the age of 18, even if the students are minors. All communication from CCCs must be directly with the students even if the students are dually enrolled in high school. However, Individualized Education Programs (IEPs) will be accepted at CCCs.

FINANCIAL RESPONSIBILITIES

DuE classes for California high school students are free at all CCCs. The website, QUOTTLY.COM, the California Community College (CCC) search engine, lists the full price of classes for college students but the amount will be adjusted in the CCC registration portal. Students will, however, be charged for text book and other course materials. Out-of-state students will be charged full price for DuE classes and materials.

BROWSE AND SEARCH FOR DUAL ENROLLMENT CLASSES

QUOTTLY.COM uses an algorithm to search all available CCC classes. There is a student registration function on QUOTTLY.COM but it is not intended for high school students as enrolling in a DuE at a CCC is a manual process. High school students must register and enroll in DuE classes directly with the specific CCC providing the DuE classes.

The easiest way to find classes that might transfer to most four year institutions is to search by selecting UC Berkeley or UC Los Angeles as "YOUR UNIVERSITY". When searching by "GEN ED REQUIREMENT" there is an option to choose the IGETC (breadth) classes by category. Use additional search functions to select different criteria and define results.

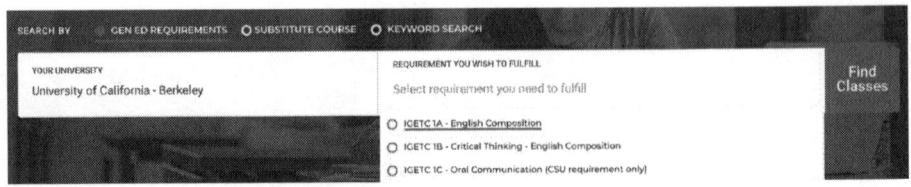

If fulfilling a breadth or a GE requirement is not the top priority, selecting a class using "KEYWORD" is helpful. For example, search "nutrition" or "sports" and there will be many CCC classes to choose from. The class description will indicate if the class is transferable to "YOUR UNIVERSITY" as an IGETC breadth or an elective. It will also indicate if the class is only transferrable to a CSU, as opposed to a UC, or not transferrable at all to a California four year institution.

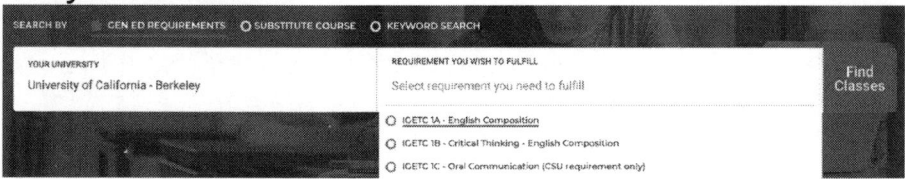

DuE classes can be in-person, online, or hybrid. Use the search functions on QUOTTLY.COM to select preferences to define results. Students can enroll in online distance learning classes at any CCC, no matter the distance to students high schools. Online distance learning classes are usually asynchronous whereby students do not have to attend classes at specific times and professors do not teach by a live synchronous video format.

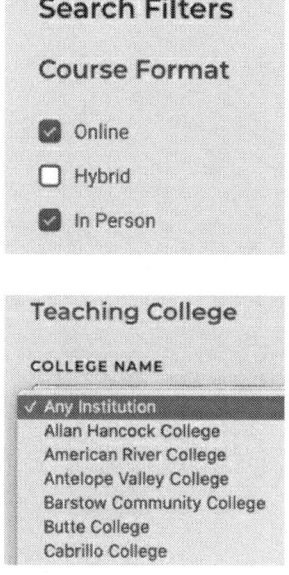

DuE classes transfer credits can verified on ASSIST.ORG, the official transfer and articulation system for California's public colleges and universities.

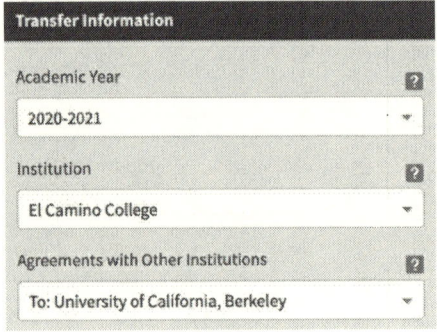

10 STEPS TO REGISTER FOR DUAL ENROLLMENT CLASSES

1. **APPLY** to the desired CCC using the portal found on the CCC website. Each CCC has a different portal and they are not linked. Only currently enrolled college students, not high school students, can use the linked registration portal on QUOTTLY.COM.

2. Receive an email with a **STUDENT ID NUMBER** and a CCC **STUDENT EMAIL ADDRESS** confirming registration.

3. If the DuE class needs **PRE-APPROVAL** from a faculty member, email the academic dean of the department for a pre-approval code or a signed Pre-approval Form (Appendix Form 1). If a **PRE-REQUISITE** course is required, complete the CCC Pre-Requisite Form located on the CCC website. Pre-approval and pre-requisite information for each course is listed on the course information page on QUOTTLY.COM If the forms are not accessible, contact the dual enrollment office at the CCC.

4. Download and complete the **CCC DuE FORM** located on the CCC website. If the form is not accessible, contact the dual enrollment office at the CCC. (Appendix Form 2)

5. Request the **HIGH SCHOOL DuE FORM** provided by the student's high school guidance counselor. (Appendix Form 3)

6. Email the **COMPLETED FORMS**, the CCC DuE Form and the High School DuE Form (with the student's section completed), to the student's high school guidance counselor for a signature.

7. Upon receipt, **UPLOAD** all of the signed forms to the CCC portal, or **EMAIL** them the CCC dual enrollment office as per directions on the CCC website.

8. The dual enrollment office at the CCC will **MANUALLY APPROVE** the student's request to enroll in the DuE class(es) on the forms. The student usually will not receive an email that the approval is complete. When the student is approved to register for the requested classes, they can continue with step 10. Therefore, the CCC portal should be checked daily to see if the approval is posted. Contact the dual enrollment office if the student is not approved after a week.

9. Confirm the student's **REGISTRATION DATE** on the CCC portal. DuE students can register for classes at CCCs after their assigned registration date which is always after new and continuing college students. If the CCC does not allow high school students to register until the waitlist period is complete (after the class has begun), the student might want to look into another CCC or have multiple classes in mind as backups.

10. **ENROLL** in the DuE class(es) on the CCC portal. If the DuE request was approved by the dual enrollment office, the student will be able to continue with class registration. Typically a student will not receive an email confirming their registered classes as they are posted on the CCC

portal.

APPENDIX

Form 1

Prerequisite Clearance Form

This form is intended for students who have taken courses at another college or university and need that course to meet a prerequisite course at El Camino College

*** INCOMPLETE FORMS LACKING REQUIRED DOCUMENTATION WILL NOT BE PROCESSED***

Name *

[First Name] [Last Name]

El Camino College ID# *

Email *

What semester and year is the clearance for? *

For example, Summer 2019; Fall 2019

Instructions: Before you submit this petition you must:

1. Complete an application to El Camino College.

2. Complete this form and attach appropriate documentation.

3. Email or mail this form and attach appropriate documentation.

Note: Please allow for 3 business days for a response. You will be notified via the email that you provided on this form.

What option will you use to clear this prerequisite? *

Form 2

 **Dual Enrollment Application**

educational opportunities for all individuals, regardless of race, color, ancestry, religion, gender, national origin, marital status, sexual orientation, handicap, age, and Vietnam-era status.

PLEASE PRINT ALL INFORMATION CLEARLY

Section I: Student Information   Semester: Summer___ Fall___ Winter___ Spring___ Year_____

El Camino College ID # ☐☐☐☐☐☐☐

Name_____ Birth Date ___/___/___ Age ____
   Last   First   MI

Address: _____ Email: _____

City: _____ State: _____ Zip: _____ Phone # _____

I have read and understand the expectations and responsibilities section on page the back of this application.

Student Signature_____ Date _____

High School: _____ (Students enrolled in a Home Study Program must provide proof that the Home Study Program is registered with the State of California).

At the time of ECC enrollment, I will be in grade 9th/10th/11th / 12th (circle one) and in the HS **Graduating Class of 20____**

Section II: Parent Consent
I have read and understand the expectations and responsibilities on page 2 this application and agree to all the conditions. I hereby give my consent to my son/daughter to attend El Camino College and enroll in the classes for which a recommendation has been made. *She/He ___does___ ___does not___ need accommodations at El Camino College due to disability. (*Students who need accommodations due to disability should make arrangements for these through their school districts in consultation with the Special Resource Center at El Camino College).

Parent Signature_____ **Print Name**_____ **Date**_____

Section III: Principal or Designee Course Recommendation
I recommend that the above named student enroll in the course(s) listed below. *For summer only: I certify the student has availed himself/herself of all opportunities to enroll in an equivalent course at his/her school of attendance, and his/her participation does not cause our school to exceed the 5 percent statutory limit. (Enrollment is limited to 2 classes. Written permission from your school is required, along with approval from El Camino College's Director of Admissions, to enroll in more than two classes).*

Course #1_____ Course #2_____

Authorized Signature_____ **Print Name**_____ **Date**_____

Section IV: Additional Approvals if Required
Registrar / Designee Approval Required To Enroll in More Than Two Classes

_____ Date _____
Registrar/Designee

Division Dean Approval for Special K/10 Admits

_____ Date _____

_____ Date _____

_____ Date _____
ECC Admissions Office Us

JEANNIE KARLITZ

Form 3

ABOUT THE AUTHOR

Jeannie Karlitz is a masters candidate at the American College of Education and is expected receive her Master of Higher Education degree in February, 2021. She wrote this handbook after her boys experienced the manual and cumbersome process of registering for dual enrollment classes at California Community Colleges.

Jeannie lives in Los Angeles County with her family and can be found on LinkedIn.

JEANNIE KARLITZ

Made in the USA
Columbia, SC
09 August 2023

21434219R00017